Love and Kindness

A time tested secret for true happiness

by Holly Roberts Merrell

Illustrations by Galih Winduadi

Copyright © 2019 by Holly Roberts Merrell
Illustrations: Galih Winduadi

All rights reserved. No part of this book may be reproduced by any mechanical, photographic, or electronic process, or in the form of a phonographic recording; nor may it be stored in a retrieval system, transmitted, or otherwise be copied for public or private use--other than for "fair use" as brief quotations embodied in articles and reviews without prior written permission of the publisher. The intent of the author is only to offer information of a general nature to help you in your quest for emotional and spiritual well-being. In the event you use any of the information in this book for yourself, the author assumes no responsibility for your actions.

Library of Congress Control Number: 2020902154

ISBN: 978-1-951982-06-5
Digital ISBN: 978-1-951982-07-2

This is a book with principles that can bring joy, satisfaction, peace, and love into your life, no matter your age.
This is a book for ALL ages.
Do you ever find yourself down in the dumps, feeling sad, and alone?
Of course you do! We all do at times. It's just part of this life. But by applying the things taught in this book, you will see your life improve more and more everyday!
Einstein has said in short "that we are here for the sole purpose of serving others". He knew the secret!
As we serve others and help them along the way, we benefit as well. Love, kindness, and service are the keys to opening our own hearts to allow in the feelings of peace, joy, and love. As you apply these teachings, your life will improve in ways you can hardly imagine. Why not give it a try! What's there to lose?

Why is there kindness,
why is there love,
peace, joy, and happiness?
Are they sent from above?

Are they ours for the taking?
Are they ours to enjoy?
Are they meant for our lives?
For each girl and each boy?

Or are we meant to be angry?
To be sad and afraid?
To feel less than the others?
To feel used and betrayed?

No, this is not so!
We're not made to feel like this!
We are made to be joyful;
to feel happiness and bliss!

This is how we are made,
it is simply our nature.
To feel peace, joy, and love
at a level much greater.

But sometimes we let go because we're simply confused. Maybe we've been hurt, abandoned, or abused.

And so we open the door
and let those feelings in.
Instead of pushing them out,
they take over and win.

We send away joy,
and we send away peace,
and before we know it
all our good feelings decrease.

But it's hard, you may say,
to always feel good.
I wish I knew how.
I wish I understood.

Well, if you will let me,
I'll give you a clue,
to chase away those feelings
this is what I do...

Forget about myself,
at least for now.
And focus on another,
and uplift them somehow.

Do a little service
for someone in need.
Say something nice to them,
or do a good deed.

Make cookies for a bully
who is always so mean.
Help your mom do the dishes
and get the house clean.

Weed the flower bed of a widow
who lives down the street.
And while you're at it,
why not make her a treat.

Shovel the driveway
for your neighbor down the road,
who just lost a loved one.
Why not help lift their load.

Or go mow the lawn
for the person next door;
even if you don't know them
and have never met them before.

Eat lunch with a kid
who seems all alone.
Whether it's a new kid at school
or someone you've known.

Give your extra coat
to a kid who's without.
Share what you have,
that's what love's all about.

You can simply say hi
to someone on the street.
Or you can say sorry
to someone you mistreat.

You can smile real big
to someone who seems sad.
And that simple act of kindness
makes both of you feel glad.

You see, kindness isn't something
to do once in a while.
It's simply a way of life
to keep a permanent smile.

When we forget ourselves
and the problems of our own,
we actually come to find
all these good feelings have grown.

They push out the anger,
the sadness, and pain.
They send ugly feelings
right down the drain.

This feeling of love,
of happiness, and joy,
can permanently be ours
for us to enjoy.

But the secret to having them
is to give what we have.
Whether our time or our talents,
it's not really that bad.

You see, as we give to others
and take time for those in need,
we feel better ourselves,
this is almost guaranteed.

It's a law of nature,
it's a law you see.
It's a law of the universe,
which has been decreed.

When you serve others,
and show kindness and love,
that's what comes back to you;
blessings from above.

But remember we are human, and we all make mistakes. We'll have moments of anger, sadness, and hate.

But don't let them stay,
push them right out the door.
By focusing on others,
you'll win, that's for sure.

And the more that you do this
the easier it will be
to send those negative feelings
on their way, and be free.

You'll start to feel happier,
to feel more joy and peace.
And all these wonderful feelings
will begin to increase.

Deep down in your heart,
when you feel really good,
an inner peace is there
because you're doing what you should.

Books by Holly Roberts Merrell...

To learn more about the author and more in depth detail of her personal experiences regarding her books, please visit hollyrobertsmerrell.com.

www.ingramcontent.com/pod-product-compliance
Lightning Source LLC
Chambersburg PA
CBHW041818040426
42452CB00001B/16